Show Date and Time
Pam Thompson

Smith/Doorstop Books

Published 2006 by
Smith/Doorstop Books
The Poetry Business
The Studio
Byram Arcade
Westgate
Huddersfield HD1 1ND

Copyright © Pam Thompson 2006
All Rights Reserved

ISBN 1-902382-84-6
Typeset at The Poetry Business
Printed by Swiftprint, Huddersfield

The Poetry Business gratefully acknowledges the help of Arts Council England and Kirklees Metropolitan Council.

Acknowledgements

Some of these poems have previously appeared in *The North*, *Magma* and *Smiths Knoll*.

'Application for the Post of Mother Nature' was a runner-up in the BBC Wildlife Magazine Poet of the Year Competition, 2003.

'Festival of Light and Water' gained second place in the East Midlands Three Cities Poetry Competition, February 2006, and is published in the related anthology.

CONTENTS

5	Morning, Early (Highlights)
6	Crash!
7	Her Grown-Up Dress
8	Invasion
10	Hoodie Season
12	December 30th 2004
13	Application for the Post of Mother Nature
14	New Year's Day: Twice Over
15	The Fishing Competition
17	Festival of Light and Water
18	Sometimes the Sea
19	At Easter
20	Show Date and Time
21	The Talking Cure
22	Relaxation Tape
23	Night Interiors
25	The Run
26	Waiting for the Bulls
27	When it Comes
28	A Sense of Things

Spent all of his life
playing for time.
All of it.
          Roy Fisher, 'Stop'

MORNING, EARLY (HIGHLIGHTS)

I give you the Black Bank pub: firkins stacked in a yard;
in the air, rainwater, stale beer.; somebody's son,
somebody's daughter, somebody's… and this is morning:
the kind of early common to the 'seventies. Street light, yellow.
You have been sitting on that felled tree between the lovers,
before the shot or shots, before no song, and no Corporation
                              buses,
maroon and cream, nor Midland Reds which could be the name
of roses, brick red beauties, near the railway line, where,
in the summer of 1973, those shots failed to permeate the miasma
of cram, was it King John or the Gothics in triplicate?
For Mrs Macauley…The Crawl…but not Mrs Slinn
of the bee-stung eyelids nor Mr Palmer, young endangered male.
 A whistle, shush of wheels: the coal train from Keresley.
And it's Latin, Mr Holland, apoplectic, aneuristic, *Salvete*
                              Puellae,
trousers and jacket, matching shade of parchment..
You never gave a thought to the boy from your class in junior
                              school;
gapped teeth, too wide shorts. But you do now. Peering down
onto the road where the line was. Mystery of a word, *amputate*.
This morning, though, I give you a pale primrose light
like a promising sky behind white blinds on what was a bedroom
                              window.
You'll think of angel hair spun around an old-fashioned tree.
Early. A tree that once shed its needles. And it's nowhere near
                              Christmas.
This is the 'seventies. Nor anything like home.

CRASH!

That was George Best booting the ball through the screen
after scoring for the first time in colour.
That's my mum sweeping glass up into a dustpan.
Those shouts are George and my dad (also George),
beered up already, staggering down to the bookies.
That sudden cheer is the crowd.
That clatter is the laughter of George's seventeen wives and
                          three hundred
(current/recent) girlfriends as they step out like golden-
                          skinned gazelles
and those thuds, high heels landing on the carpet.
Some sit on sofas, some on the floor. Some are squashed in
                          the hallway;
Angie, Queen Bee, who'll outlast them, majestic in the
                          hearth.
That hysterical squealing is the kettle. The toilet door opens.
Out comes one of the Swedish Evas who takes a mug of tea
                          from my mother.
And that? The small sound of a punctured football hissing.

HER GROWN-UP DRESS

When she came at last to that row of shops
on the long road, having left behind the dirt track,
railway line, the sluggish brook and had fastened
round gold slides in her mud brown hair,
pulled plimsolls on her feet so the backs weren't squashed
she found the shops were boarded up, that the woman
standing there wore a pale green cotton dress,

and when the tall young man stepped from shadows
of a sealed up shop the woman's face was like a pearl
whose lustre lasted all the time she held his arm
and walked slowly down that long road which trains
hadn't crossed for years, where the brook was dry,
and the cotton dress was just a stem stripped down,
its milk pale sap evaporating in air,
and the young man a tree it had briefly leaned against.

INVASION

It began with a cold. An itch
in the nose. A twitch in the throat. A torrent
of snot like snail trail on his fingers.

Then the cough. At first, a dry tic.
Fags didn't help. Or a toke on a spliff
in the street. Except he was hooked,

fit for the inhaler, the patch or the gum.
A fever: the shakes;
his arms felt light; his legs felt numb.

Every night in his head inconsolable bees.
In his guts, a rusty crooked knife.
Bats snagged his lungs when he breathed.

>And in the dark night of his soul
>   an angel rapped,
>like Eminem, like Ice T.

>In the stark fright of the toilet bowl
>   his tea stank.
>The rest embellished his bedroom floor

>and the gutter outside his window
>   and waited
>for pigeons to peck it, rain to sluice it

>into the street, amongst leaves, sidetrack it
>   into the gutter
>so in the morning, pissing off learner drivers,

the council sweeper commandeers
        the borders of the road
will sanctify the space where it has been

while he slept, oblivious to builders, Radio 1,
        his phone alarm's panic,
his mates coming and going

and his mother's long goodbye before
        she left for work.
It wasn't the drink. He'd got a gene from his dad

that leaves him standing after eight pints,
        a couple of vodka and Red Bulls,
and the DNA of the winner on the pitch,

the jaunty right foot, the perky left heel,
        the dodge and the weave
on the court, and an eye for the ball

even at squash in a space where you couldn't
        swing a cat, can hammer it
down the fast lane in the pool.

Or did. Before this.

HOODIE SEASON

1. **Shot**

Everywhere, hoodies.
This was the season of the scare.

Cowled youths in shadows,
shot from below.

In a restricted space,
wouldn't you look dangerous
as the photographer closes in like a hunter?

2. **Your new hoodie**

Buying it, you were more concerned
about the spot on your lip;
kept glancing in shop mirrors,
fretted that it would put the girls off.

Then you dipped into your rolling
long armed, broad shouldered gait,
hormonal man-boy, *built*
but not as tall as some of your mates.

Will I get tall? I catch your smell.
Cheap hair gel, sweat, Lacoste,
bought by me duty free on a trip to Budapest
where there was no hoodie scare,

just the Danube looking famous,
statues of heroes in a public park,

and young people picking lilacs on Sunday,
to perfume their grandparents' houses.

3. Notice outside a shopping mall

You are not allowed to enter with your hood in the up position.

What might a boy in a hoodie do?
Slap you down? Kick you around?
Take a picture on his mobile phone
and send it round the school?

Or
        (Hood in the down position)

Capsize a skateboard.
Smoke some weed in a cul-de-sac.
Litter that part of the road
with an empty packet of Lambert and Butlers.

Eat chips. Go on MSN Chat
at a mate's house. Download porn.
Blowjobs in the street.
Drink a can of his mate's dad's Heineken.

        (Hood in the up position)

Walk home at eleven.
A cold wind. Two days,
then the first GCSE.
He'll wing it like he wings everything.

Bed. Hoodie on the floor
cradling his smells.
Tobacco, sweat, Lacoste.

DECEMBER 30TH 2004

Bronze leaves on pavements:
frosted brooches a summer-seeking goddess
might have dropped leaving this world
of mobile phones and fast food.

Sixteen – a day, a night,
my son downloads long-haired girls
with eyes cold as dead stars
from web-sites that might be other planets,
the women aliens.

How could those breasts ever nurture other lifeforms?

I've travelled here. Flick through albums.
Make no sense of the past.
The past as incubator, shawl,
changing mat; as pantomime (those
costumes). The ages. Stacked on the floor.

My daughter fourteen, falls in love
with her face again;
is my younger fleeing self.

Close the album. Leave my daughter
to her mirror, my son, alone,
discovering goddesses.

APPLICATION FOR THE POST OF MOTHER NATURE

Late May. The gorgeous coppery wild cherry
is shadowing the lawn. I'm typing this by desk-light,
remembering last month's hail, the lawn's crisp glaze,
and how this morning I jiggled the lock on the patio door
to look for my son's trainer. Finding it in the lilac bush,
I snatched here and there, deadheading, sampling scents.
The net was off the pond. I draped it back
and imagined the fiefdom of the ghost coy; his orange underlings;
a heron swaying in an elm two roads away.

Oh and yesterday a fox, all housebreaker's swagger,
eyeballed me then slotted himself through a neighbour's fence.

My past and present experience.

Maybe I lack desirable requirements:
am neither bosomy with tactile hands, a stay at home,
nor a wildly roaming seeker of skies and herbal lore –
not rhetorical, empyrean, unable, like Titania,
to describe this 'mazed' world with its complicated seasons.

But I'm typing this by desk-light. The cherry steps back in twilight,
her big hair still. And those are my referees, city kids, wired
from Playstation, TV, and those are their mates, tall,
white-faced, fifteen, round the pond, trainers never far
from the ball, staying near, they keep it near, sticks like a terrier,
then one voice cracking wider than the gaps in crazy paving
yelps, 'Look, a frog!'

NEW YEAR'S DAY: TWICE OVER

1981

3am. Way past Auld Lang Syne, in that pub,
over and over, Human League, 'Don't You Want Me'.

That much was true. If everyone could have been
as sure about the past as Phil Oakey especially

in the darkness to come, that holiday in Corfu
where there'd be a banging storm with power cuts

and you'd both be trapped in that rented room
for thirty-six hours. Ahead, the family

you thought you'd never have, the three of them,
ignoring you, blaming you for all that, for all this.

2000

1am. In the kitchen, dusting Christmas cake crumbs from empty
           cupboards
where you've failed to stockpile imperishables. In your road, trestle-
           tables, buntings.

Neighbours are convivial, launching Millennium rockets, but in
           other houses,
some of your friends, like you, are cheering themselves alone.

You shift a curtain but keep invisible. It's a kind of siege.
Any time now you expect shoulders against the door;

Mr Burly from number twelve to denounce you as a traitor to the
           communal
celebratory cause. Or the Millennium Bug, in person, first-footing.

THE FISHING COMPETITION

1.

I want to sit on a canal bank
but nowhere near those fishermen
and their triumphal arch of rods;
their stinking jars of maggots;
their cans of Long Life.

Before a fish is dangled
like a dark dripping slipper,
I want to be away at the next lock,
helping a pleasant elderly couple
prise the gates apart

then with them, pass, oh so slowly,
through the tidy, lovely water,
upping the engine's disruptive growl
so that the winning bite
sashays downstream

and the maggot on each line's untasted
though the pool we leave behind
will be stared at, sifted,
long after the women at home
have packed up and moved on.

2.

It's entirely Zen, this waiting. It's the quality
of waiting that counts in the end,
to tame the monkey mind,
the human tendency to shake, to twitch.
The synaptic response to a flicker of wind
on a line, the mock bite of weed, tease of
a current.
        Let your mind flow and flower
like the hawthorn blossom on the bank.
He who waits will be rewarded.

People on narrow boats call:
Caught any yet? or *What's the point?*
You'll explain yet again that the point
isn't in what's pulled out
but in what's thrown back.

You're reassured when your neighbour
a few feet away does exactly the same as you.
And the light fades. And the midges
dance stir crazy across the skin of things.
You want to feel it one more time.
You can't even see the end of your line.
You suspect this is the nearest you'll ever get to love.

FESTIVAL OF LIGHT AND WATER

Second only to celebrations in Mumbai
crowds block the Belgrave Road at Divali
to see the sky explode; to greet
an aunt or sister, not forgotten but rarely
met except in photos in Walsall or in Oadby.
A traveller ties up his narrow boat at Belgrave Lock,
émigré from the South. It's taken him a week
to get here: time out from the clock.
Behind, a frieze of anglers; in each line-flick
irritation or something stronger. Brisk
frills of water where sudden snakes flip backwards
from canal to sky; restless coils
that wriggle up through weeds and oil. Squeals;
glove tight, pink fingered cochineal sheathes
of fire unfurling like skin that peels.
Some share rose lassi. Some throw rose petals down
from the bridge. Tomorrow he'll unpick garlands
from the propeller, kick a spent rocket in
an unwinding swathe of water,
and will pass, hand on tiller,
just here, on this symbolic Ganges, a spent pyre:
rice and jasmine, framed by splints of balsa
floating on a plastic lily-pad from Asda.
As he passes, rods will quiver like saplings;
trees redouble via their reflections.
Maggots will sink and tense jaws soften
and circles inside circles widen
as weeds unfurl a carp or tench and the day lengthens.

SOMETIMES THE SEA

There's always an horizon,
unless it's night
and the sky will always
have something in it,
whether stars, clouds,
or a plane in which some of us
will be looking out
and down, speculating
whether it's better to crash
in water or on land.

And sometimes there'll be houses,
little hives which cling to rocks,
with whose buzzing
activities we'll never interact,
and usually waves
will flick white fists and fingers,
and often lights,
which we'll name with
the first thing inhabiting
our minds –
bead, eye, planet,

sister, pain,
and even though we think we hear it
being transmitted via
our held-up shoe, a rolled up newspaper,
or ragged half of a plastic bottle,
it's never the sea
but our own thoughts,
starting small, then swelling.

AT EASTER

Grey stone, pebble dashed;
at the front, a drive, three cars.
At the back, a terraced lawn;
a gate; rotting steps; an estuary
which is sometimes a river;
sometimes a stream you can wade across.

The beach is from early childhood –
the first footprints, or rather trainer prints,
in the morning, yours. The sea even smells of sea –
weedy, coconut oiled.

At first there's nothing to scare you.

But then a biker blasts past; teenage boys,
brown chests bared, spring from a dune,
say get off their fucking turf.

Relatives are watching from the safe house –
look up, you can't see them.
Windows are blank grey water.

Now, the river bends.
You are between the sand dunes and the sea.
Now they have lost you.

SHOW DATE AND TIME

Since then
> they have cut down the trees behind the house,
> cumulus clouds are more prevalent in the neighbourhood
> and unknown animals pace the outlying fields.
>
> There is new legislation against rambling; there
> is new legislation about not scrawling your name
> in indelible marker on the nearest street sign

>> but you do.

Since that time

> the hallway has become overgrown with flyers,
> letters, newspapers and a loose ball of garden twine
> which you unwind still further, tie to the valve of a radiator

>> walking into the rest of your life,

> holding onto the end holding on so that if, when, soon
> you can rewind, trace your way back to the street sign where
> your hectic scrawl reminds you who you were.

THE TALKING CURE

Budapest. An island park. Young couples pulling down lilacs
to offer grandparents as compensation for being old.
And you are telling her this. From your mouth. *Lilacs*.

From your lips. *Old*. Fifty pounds an hour
in an inner city room as five o' clock traffic
poisons the air. You know the temperature

on the side of the newspaper building will be ten degrees
warmer than in reality. She has lit an incense cone
without your permission. She is burning vanilla,

green tea, blackberry, or maybe lilac.
She reminds you of Paul Weller, particularly around the eyes
and hairline. You want to confess some dark sin

that she'd absolve but your mind wanders,
for at least twenty three pounds, back to the Danube
and speculates on why it was ever regarded as blue.

RELAXATION TAPE

Today, a rainforest, a tinkling waterfall, melodic whistling
of parakeets – or are they cockatoos?
He calls to her but his voice is far away.
Liannas are thick, varicose. If she should trip.
Where is she? Sarawak? One moment he was beside her
like a doctor full of bedside manner
now he's rowing towards her in a hollowed out canoe
on a river at dusk where fireflies jig .

No, she still feels mental. This is not Borneo
but a shit infested dump. There goes her office in flames.
She steps over clumps of rubble; varicose cables.
Flies ping her face and he rows down
a black canal chanting numbers backwards.
She will not repeat them. She will not lift her left hand.
She is not feeling sleepy. She can still feel her toes
and all of her fingers – that splayed span of multi-coloured feathers.

NIGHT INTERIORS

1. The Pub

Looking across the A6, at 4am, through rain,
at first nothing lit up for the latch of your gaze
to drop onto only somebody wading
through shadows, and the name of the pub,
The Owl, in fact, not in any kind of flight
but hunched between golf course and college,
then that window, a frame, its stretched canvas,
yellow/white; an arm, now a shoulder, against glass;
the blotch of a cap, a cue. The further you step back
the more it clarifies, a print of young men
crouched over baize. Step forward, as if to tap
on a pane, see it blur; watch its colours run.

2. The Museum

There's nothing to wake; they're long dead,
just bones of the Brachiosaurus,
hauled upright, as if it were feasting
on trees in a primeval forest.
Trilobites are boxed; the shrew, glassy-eyed
like the bear; twisted on stiff wires, the hare.
Pretend moonlight sticks to labels
on cabinets where moths pretend to fly.
Paintings upstairs have to be guessed at.
That is, until the eye with its night sight widens
at Lizzy Siddal, beatific in furs;
a Cavalier on a horse, dark on dark;
smudge of moon by Samuel Palmer.
Anyone can touch them now;
lick a finger, alter a master's design.

Miniature dragnets of light sweep the chair
of an attendant who, at home, is not asleep
but surfing for a holiday in Costa Rica.
The café is distinctly closed;
smells of coffee, lavender floor polish.
There is no-one to wake. No-one who stays;
no-one to shake from sleep at a table,
 head on arms like a child bored with school.
No-one to paint; no-one to cover with furs.

3. The Petrol Station

Early Easter eggs nose out of boxes.
Santok will start the display tonight
when the grilles go up, sorting Cadbury's Crème
from Terry's Gold. Ever prescient, Santok,
of the next big thing: sledges if it snows;
Red Noses; charcoal for summer barbies.
Until gone eight queues stretched up Welford Road,
past the Martial Arts Superstore, the post office,
as far as the poet streets, Herrick, Byron,
Keats, but now, 11pm, panic's over.
Rumours of blockades have proved a fiction.
Santok brings in flowers, empties tubs,
refills them, twitching cellophane
under blue strip lighting. Going and coming,
redoubled in the chestnut flank
of a customised Subaru,
he steps towards himself; breaks away,

THE RUN

> *The crew of the Shuttle Columbia did not return safely to
> Earth; yet we can pray that all are safely home.*
> President G W Bush, 1st February 2003

You run, or start to, taking on the night again.
Muggers can't harm you when you have earphones in
tuned to Rap FM, pressing buttons through your gloves,

then something classical. A phone-in.
You are running off doors slamming; being
crushed between voices like a fly between fingernails.

That plane could be a hurled star and the moon
is identifiably the same as that beamed back
from the jinxed shuttle where astronauts

pointed at favourite constellations, Perseus,
one woman's choice: a hero securing a bride
as reward for his trials. Those pitiful stars,

you think, walking the last bit, past the garage,
your own windows, whose light-boxes house curious experiments
of an earthly kind relating to fathers and sons

and then there are choices – turn the key in the door,
stretch your limbs in the hall, or run, earphones
back in, past negatives of trees and cars.

WAITING FOR THE BULLS

The first comes tamely like a saint.
        His eyes are calm. His fur is white

as sanctity. He licks my palm and a faint
        sound of birdsong, a smell of earth, rises

from where his hooves have been. Gentle.
        Not like the second. His horns have a scythe's

curl. When he stamps and snorts the land
        buckles, olive groves burn. *Tell*

me, I entreat, *of your pain*. But there
        is no reason in him. The third walks

like a dancer, is womanly yet
        his man's heart is visible like a lit-up globe.
The last is a typical bull. He dies at my feet.
.

WHEN IT COMES

It will not be seismic, but subtle like scent;
windows won't break, the earth won't shift.
As unobtrusive as a leaf in March
it will barely flicker, a tense green tongue.

When it comes you may hear irregular beats,
like a faulty pentameter, a leaky heart.
One of seven plots, you will act in it, I will act.
We will catch our breaths. Lean forwards

in a theatre from the gods with no optical device,
no extra device, to view it. You may not
even hear it as it won't be seismic but subtle.
Like scent. Like a leaf. Near your lips as you move to kiss it.

A SENSE OF THINGS

This time of year and you're there again
to find the front door even more swollen,
hardly a sign of green paint
and water in puddles like dirty glass;
glass in the windows like mud-spattered water.

You have returned then to a plain sense of some things.
The flowering cherry still tries to balance
its last pale gold leaves and you prise open
the side gate as you do every year,
go round the back to your kitchen table,
now almost black, or rather, to that shrine
with three objects, witness to how time was then,
is now: a doorbell with wires attached;
a soapstone; a tennis ball, halved.